Original title:
What Do the Elves Do?

Copyright © 2024 Creative Arts Management OÜ
All rights reserved.

Author: Alexander Thornton
ISBN HARDBACK: 978-9916-90-848-8
ISBN PAPERBACK: 978-9916-90-849-5

Threads of Illumination in the Dark

In shadows deep, they stitch their dreams,
With glimmering threads that twist and gleam.
They sneak and peek, with mischief to spark,
Creating bright tales in the silent dark.

With tiny hammers, they craft a tune,
While tap-dancing softly like little raccoons.
Their giggles echo like a jolly lark,
As they weave their magic in the night's arc.

Secrets Written in Dewy Petals

On petals fine, they scribe their notes,
In invisible ink, with butterfly coats.
They whisper secrets only flowers know,
While plotting ways to make their friends glow.

A traipse through gardens, each sprout a spy,
With jokes and pranks that make daisies sigh.
Their laughter dances through the morning air,
As they trade tales with napping mice fair.

Elven Lullabies in the Ferns

In the ferns, a gentle tune,
Where sleepy critters sway like a balloon.
They croon to stars with a whispering hum,
While tickling the toes of a sleepy drum.

Each lullaby is spun from glee,
Filling the night with sweet jubilee.
They mix up rhymes in a frolicking swirl,
As fluttering fireflies light up their whirl.

The Arcane Playgrounds of Woodland Folk

In tangled woods, with trees that play,
The woodland folk laugh throughout the day.
They climb on branches, swing like a kite,
And slide down roots, what a silly sight!

With acorn caps as hats so fine,
They have grand feasts of berry and wine.
They challenge squirrels to races and cheer,
Creating chaos, spreading joy and cheer.

Guardians of the Hidden Realm

In the shadows, they twirl and spin,
Crafting mischief, with giggles akin.
Tiptoeing quietly, in boots made of fluff,
Chasing each other, just being enough.

With acorn hats and a wink so sly,
They plot little pranks as time flutters by.
Hiding behind toadstools, they burst with glee,
Nature's own jesters, wild and free.

The Artistry of Starlit Weavings

With webs of light spun from moonlit dreams,
They braid the night with bright silver beams.
Each stitch a laugh, each knot a jest,
In laughter they twine, never a rest.

Plucking at stars with delicate grace,
Chasing them down, a shimmering race.
Between the laughter and twinkling fun,
They weave the night until rises the sun.

Songs of the Ancient Oak

Beneath the old oak, in whispers so sweet,
They gather around for a whimsical beat.
Singing of acorns and mushrooms that dance,
With every note, they spin in a trance.

The branches sway gently, keeping the time,
As laughter erupts in a comical rhyme.
Perhaps they'll share tales of shoes made of leaves,
Tickling the branches, as nature believes.

Delicate Hands and Daring Dreams

With tiny hands crafting wonders unseen,
They mold the world into something serene.
Creating bright toys made of twigs and cheer,
Each trinket a treasure, each giggle a dear.

From flower pot hats to ribbons of light,
Their passions ignite, like dancing in flight.
Bold in their schemes, yet gentle in play,
They sprinkle the woods with joy every day.

Moonbeam Messengers of the Night

In the quiet, they flit and glide,
Whispers carried on the tide.
With giggles bright as the moon's glow,
They play tag with shadows below.

Sprinkling stardust on sleeping logs,
Dancing around with cheerful frogs.
An orchestra of twinkling chimes,
In a world woven of dreams and rhymes.

Tales from the Glittering Dell

In the dell, mischief's afoot,
Elves in boots, oh what a hoot!
With acorn hats and berry treats,
They have picnics, sharing sweets.

Tiny pranks with marshmallow goo,
Making the forest giggle, too.
They weave tales of laughter and joy,
Every twig a toy for the boy.

Echoes of Merriment in Hidden Hollows

In hollows where shadows dance,
Elves weave chaos, given the chance.
With bubblegum threads and wild glee,
They craft landscapes for you and me.

Mushroom hats and jolly songs,
Jests that echo where joy belongs.
As whispers of giggles take flight,
They sprinkle fun through the night.

Elven Hands Crafting the Stars

With tiny hands and twinkly eyes,
They stitch the stars, oh what a surprise!
Each constellation tastes like cake,
And laughter echoes with every shake.

Playing hopscotch on beams of light,
They giggle and twirl, oh what a sight!
Crafting wishes, one by one,
Under the watch of the playful sun.

Dreamweavers of the Greenheart Realm

In a glade where giggles soar,
Elves weave dreams that float and roar.
With threads of laughter, bright and wide,
They stitch the joy that can't abide.

With paintbrushes made of dew and light,
They splash the mornings, sparkling bright.
A tickle here, a sparkle there,
For smiles grow wildly everywhere!

The Hidden Life Beneath the Canopy

Beneath the leaves, they scurry and dart,
With mischief wrapped around their heart.
They have tea with squirrels, toast with bees,
And plan their pranks with giggles and wheeze.

When moonlight dances on grassy beds,
Elves spin tales while resting their heads.
With every whisper, secrets unfold,
In the depths of night, it's pure gold.

Dance of the Twinkling Fireflies

In moonlit fields, their shoes are bright,
They trip the grass with pure delight.
A jig with fireflies, they take a chance,
In a swirling, twirling, glowing dance.

They chuckle and tumble, oh what a sight,
As the stars join in their merry flight.
With bubbles of laughter filling the air,
They prance and play without a care.

Symphony of the Sylvan Spirits

A symphony plays in the forest deep,
Where the elves dance softly, without a peep.
With flutes made of bark and drums from the ground,
They create a rhythm that's joyfully found.

They sing to the flowers, and twirl with the breeze,
Stirring up giggles with absolute ease.
For in their world, laughter is key,
As they entertain all of nature's glee!

Guardians of the Age-Old Oak

Beneath the ancient, twisted tree,
A gathering of elves in glee.
They argue over acorn hats,
And dance with squeaky rubber rats.

One elf juggles pine cones with flair,
While others nap on mossy chairs.
They giggle at the squirrels' squeaks,
And share their snacks of peanut tweaks.

Alchemy of Enchantment in the Glade

In the glade where magic flows,
Elves measure herbs in silly rows.
They brew a potion that turns toads,
Into squeaky boots on winding roads.

With a wink and a flash of light,
They let the frogs take off in flight.
But oops! A potion's gone all wrong,
Now log frogs sing a silly song!

The Festival of Flora and Fauna

At dawn, the elves start up their games,
With flower crowns and funny names.
They race the rabbits, quick and spry,
While juggling daisies flying high.

A hedgehog judges the pastry bake,
With tortes made of mushroom cake.
They cheer for bloom, each bud and leaf,
As bees join in, beyond belief!

Hues of Enchantment in the Meadow

In a meadow bright with color and cheer,
Elves paint the flowers, oh so dear.
They mix up hues like wild, mad cooks,
And laugh when cows walk off with books.

A butterfly joins in the fun,
In a swirling dance under the sun.
They giggle as the colors run,
And paint their faces—what a pun!

Magpies of Magic and Mirth

In the forest, laughter bubbles,
Magpies dance in strange huddles.
With a wink and a cheeky grin,
Juggling acorns, let the fun begin.

They toss around glittering leaves,
Making mischief, oh, how it weaves!
Silly spells and juggling tricks,
As the branches sway and flicks.

In teacups, they sip sweet dew,
Swapping tales, both old and new.
With tiny hats made of moss,
They're the magpies, never at a loss.

Echoes of laughter fill the air,
Mirth and magic, everywhere!
Join the fun, but tread with care,
For these magpies are quite the rare!

In the Presence of Celestial Beings

Beneath the moon, a giggle floats,
Celestial beings ride on goats.
With starry hats and shoes of light,
They twirl and prance, oh, what a sight!

In silken robes, they twirl and sway,
Chasing fireflies, come out to play.
Each flicker a wish, a tiny spark,
In this nighttime revelry, oh, what a lark!

Whispers of chaos spun with glee,
As they dance round the ancient tree.
With strawberry dreams and passion fruit,
Their spirit's contagious, oh, what a hoot!

So if you hear a titter or two,
Know celestial beings are not through.
Join their fest, jump up and shout,
For laughter echoes, there's no doubt!

The Folly of Fireflies and Elves

In the dusk, the fireflies twirl,
Elves jump high in quite a whirl.
Their tiny shoes are made for fun,
Glowing brightly, they outrun the sun.

With a lantern made of dandelion,
They flit about, a colorful science.
One bumps a leaf, and what a mess,
A pile of giggles, in their happy dress.

They play hopscotch on moonlit beams,
Floating in clouds like swirling dreams.
With ivy crowns and berry pies,
They're the silliest sprites under starry skies.

Sharing secrets, chuckling loud,
Mischief sparks a gathering crowd.
When night falls, oh boy, beware,
For the folly of elves is everywhere!

Echoes of the Giggles in the Grove

In the grove, echoes ring clear,
Giggling sprites, come closer, my dear.
They play hide and seek in the vines,
Beneath the twinkling, shimmering pines.

With a swift dash and a playful poke,
They peek from trees, each giggle a joke.
Their antics spread joy from tree to tree,
Such magic and laughter, what glee to see!

Wearing crowns made of shamrock green,
They prance about, the happiest seen.
With mischief running wild and free,
In the grove's embrace, laughter's decree.

So join the fun, let your spirit flow,
In the giggling grove, let your joy grow.
For each leap and bound, they invite with cheer,
Echoes of laughter, forever near!

When the Fireflies Gather

In skies of twilight, they twinkle like stars,
Elves giggle and dance, beneath moonlit guitars.
With tiny green hats and mismatched bright shoes,
They serve up some nectar and drink chilly brews.

Around the old oak, they hold a grand feast,
Where laughter and mischief tame even the beast.
With snacks made of acorns and puddles of cream,
They serenade fireflies, chanting a dream.

Echoes of Enchantment in the Night

In the heart of the forest, with mischief afoot,
Elves whisper their secrets while stomping in soot.
They tickle the ferns, and they tussle with moss,
Making raucous remarks that leave squirrels at cross.

A bucket of giggles spills down from the trees,
Creating a ruckus that carries on the breeze.
As shadows do glide, and the night sings its tune,
They duel with the owls, beneath a bright moon.

Guardians of the Whispering Woods

With hats made of petals and smiles of delight,
The guardians frolic through enchanted twilight.
They giggle with hedgehogs and bounce with the deer,
Tickling the roots, they spread joy far and near.

Catching the giggles of rabbits in flight,
They throw lavish parties until morning light.
From toadstools of velvet, they serve berry pies,
And toast to the stars, with mischief in their eyes.

Tread Softly on Elven Pathways

Tread lightly, dear friends, on paths paved with glee,
Where elves chase the shadows of sweet silvered trees.
They slip on the mushrooms and giggle with frogs,
Playing tag with the whispers and hug all the logs.

They weave with the breeze, chasing whispers of air,
And snickering softly with wild, maned hair.
In a tangle of moonbeams, they roll and they spin,
With laughter like bubbles that never grow thin.

Whispers in the Moonlit Glade

In the night, they jump around,
Twirling, spinning, what a sound!
With acorns tossed and hats askew,
They laugh and giggle—oh, who knew?

Sprightly dances near the stream,
Chasing fireflies, living the dream.
A hop, a skip, a playful tease,
In moonlight's glow, they do as they please.

Winking stars are their best friends,
On secret paths, the mischief blends.
Crafting crowns from leaves so neat,
And finding snacks that are a treat.

Beneath the branches, whispers sway,
In lilting tones, they plot their play.
With sneaky grins and sparkly shoes,
They steal the socks we didn't choose.

The Secret Lives of Woodland Sprites

In the shadows, quick they flit,
Sprinkling laughter, never sit.
With tiny pranks, they stir the air,
Leaving giggles everywhere.

Under mushrooms, they do reside,
In acorn homes, their dreams abide.
A tiny feast of berry jam,
A silly dance to cats' 'meow' spam.

Tickling trees and teasing snails,
They craft their nets from willow trails.
In secret meetings, plans are made,
To paint the night with glitter's jade.

When morning comes, they sneak away,
In dawn's first light, they drift and sway.
With whispers soft, their voices draw,
A funny world without a flaw.

Elven Craft Beneath the Stars

With twinkling eyes, they start to weave,
Brighting leaves on which they cleave.
Gathering threads of starlit dew,
Stitching tales of wondrous view.

Beneath the oak, they build a boat,
From sweetened sap and misty groat.
They sail through dreams on currents high,
Chasing whispers in the sky.

They paint the rocks with cheery hues,
And leave behind some wiggly clues.
In twilight's glow, they laugh with glee,
Creating havoc, wild and free.

When the sun starts to poke its head,
They hide the mischief that they spread.
With sparkly notes, they tend to go,
Leaving laughter in the flow.

Twilight Mischiefs of the Fey

As the day bids night farewell,
They gather 'round with tales to tell.
With tiny sparkles in the air,
They plot a prank without a care.

Toadstool hats and fairy wings,
They dance and jive to silly things.
With every leap, a chuckle bursts,
In harmony with woodland thirsts.

A spritz of fun, a pinch of gleam,
Making stars from their delight theme.
While we just wonder what they might,
They wave their wands and blur the sight.

When morning glows, their giggles fade,
But traces of their fun are laid.
In every rustling leaf and song,
The fey's humor lingers long.

The Art of Twilight Crafting

Twilight falls, a spark of light,
Tiny hands, in glee, take flight.
Crafting wonders, oh so neat,
Bottled giggles, a joyful treat.

Their laughter dances on the breeze,
Painting colors in the trees.
With each snip and each swirl,
They make the night a dazzling whirl.

Mischievous Makers of Marvels

Bouncing on toadstools, oh so spry,
Mischief twinkles in their eye.
They twirl the wands to cast a laugh,
While baking pies that make you gaff.

Juggling berries, a fruity show,
Filling mugs with frothy hello.
Silly songs that make no sense,
Can turn a frown to pure pretense.

Revelry in the Hidden Grove

In the grove, the music flows,
Hiding secrets, nobody knows.
Elfin giggles make the stars blink,
As they dance on the edge of pink.

Glimmering leaves, a secret stage,
Picking wildflowers, they engage.
Twirling in circles, they can't contain,
The joy that bubbles like champagne.

Sprites at Play

Sprites at play, oh what a sight,
Climbing up the mushrooms, such delight.
Swinging on vines, they share a cheer,
Painting the clouds with lots of beer.

With little hats and shoes so bright,
They cast spells that twinkle at night.
Chasing fireflies, a glowing chase,
They fill the dark with a happy grace.

Beneath the Stars

Beneath the stars, they plot and scheme,
Sipping nectar, living the dream.
Swaps of candy 'neath moonlit skies,
With giggles that tickle and never die.

Little whispers, secrets shared,
With mischief, they're unabashedly spared.
Crafting a world where laughter reigns,
In silly antics, joy remains.

The Mischief of Moonlit Shadows

Beneath the moon, they play all night,
With twinkling eyes, a comical sight.
They trip on mushrooms, they giggle and dash,
Creating chaos, a joyful splash.

In the garden, they steal a sock,
Watch out for pranks around the clock!
They ride on fireflies, zooming so fast,
Leaving giggles in their sparkling past.

With tiny hands, they toss the leaves,
And play tag with the soft autumn breeze.
They hide in thickets, just out of view,
Plotting their next silly rendezvous.

At dawn, they scatter like morning dew,
As sunlight warms, they bid adieu.
But come nightfall, with laughter they'll creep,
Whispering tales while the world's asleep.

A Tapestry of Light and Laughter

Tiny figures weave in delight,
Crafting wonders in the soft moonlight.
With sugar and giggles, they spin and twirl,
Creating a feast, causing hearts to whirl.

Their laughter echoes through the trees,
As they dance on petals, fueled by the breeze.
Tangled in ribbons of sparkling gold,
Making mischief, they never grow old.

They fill the night with whimsy and cheer,
Mixing stardust with giggles, oh dear!
The fairies, they set up a carnival spree,
With games and prizes, oh what glee!

But beware, once dawn leads the way,
They vanish like mist, come break of day.
Leaving behind a wink and a sigh,
Their laughter lingers, as they say goodbye.

They Who Dance with the Wind

In the glen, they chase swirling leaves,
With twirls and spins, as the autumn grieves.
Each gust brings giggles, with twinkly grins,
While the world above quietly spins.

They ride the breezes, up high and down low,
With whispers of secrets the trees seem to know.
They tickle the clouds, a playful pursuit,
Wearing crowns made of wildflower loot.

Their games are a riddle, spun of feather and thread,
Leaving laughter trailing in places they tread.
They turn every shadow into a playmate,
Giggling softly at their merry fate.

But when the sun rises, they bounce out of sight,
In a flash, they vanish, oh what a delight!
Yet come sunset, with the stars to descend,
They'll dance in the twilight, their revelry won't end.

Threads of Gold in the Dark

With threads of gold, they stitch the night,
Crafting laughter that glimmers bright.
Each tangle brings smiles, a joyful surprise,
As they weave their magic under the skies.

They tuck away stars in pockets so deep,
While crafting soft giggles that never shall sleep.
With mischief in their hearts, they twirl and they play,
Transforming the night into a grand ballet.

They toss moonbeams like scattered confetti,
Causing the raccoons to dance all unsteady.
Chasing shadows and blushing with glee,
Creating a world that's wondrous and free.

But as dawn tiptoes, they scurry away,
Hiding their laughter till the next fun day.
With threads of joy, their mischief ignites,
In dreams, we remember their playful nights.

In the Realm Where Dreams Take Flight

In the glen where giggles bloom,
Tiny folk with brooms will zoom.
They juggle stars and paint the skies,
While whispering secrets that tickle the wise.

With hats too big and shoes too wide,
They dance on mushrooms, full of pride.
With a hop and a skip, they sing out loud,
Declaring mischief, oh so proud!

In the realm where wishes grow,
They prank the shadows, steal the show.
Riding leaves that swirl and twirl,
Each little elf gives fate a whirl!

The Artist of Midnight's Canvas.

Underneath the silver glow,
An artist paints with moonlit flow.
With a brush made of spider silk,
He colors dreams like creamy milk.

His palette's full of starry night,
And laughter echoes, pure delight.
He splashes wishes on the stream,
Creating chaos from a dream!

Every stroke a funny tale,
Of cheese that dances, and fish that sail.
But when the dawn begins to peek,
He hides his art, lest dreams grow weak!

Whispers in the Moonlit Glade

In the glade where shadows play,
Elves whisper secrets day by day.
With tiny cups filled with dew,
They brew up giggles, just for you.

They hear the trees and tickle the breeze,
With jokes and riddles that aim to please.
Through rustling leaves, the laughter flows,
As they share tales nobody knows.

When night falls down and stars align,
The elves invent a silly sign.
"Beware the flowers that start to dance!"
And off they go, in a prancing trance!

Starlit Secrets of the Woodfolk

In the woods where secrets thrive,
Woodfolk giggle, fun and jive.
They hand out gumdrops on a tree,
And dare the rabbits to dance with glee.

With acorn hats and beetle shoes,
They sing the songs only whimsies choose.
Creating mischief without a care,
As the moonlight winks, daring them to dare.

Their pranks are silly, never mean,
They paint the meadow with jellybean green.
With giggles that ricochet through the night,
These woodfolk charm with pure delight!

The Timeless Jests of Little Folk

In the twilight's gentle embrace,
Little folk dance with a grin,
Stealing socks from a quiet place,
Tickling toes of sleepy kin.

With winks and nods, they sneak around,
Hiding sweets in the glovebox,
Laughing hard at the silly sound,
Kazoo bands playing with no socks.

They turn mud into little pies,
And ring the bells of a tiny cat,
With jests and giggles, they devise,
A game of chase with a hat.

Under moonlight, they take a ride,
On leaves that sail through the air,
With a merry tune that won't subside,
The world's their stage, full of flair.

Enchantment in the Hushed Silence

In quiet corners, mischief brews,
Where shadows sway with expert glee,
They swap the coffee for honeyed brew,
And leave a note that's signed, 'Hee-hee!'

With secrets soft as evening's sigh,
They sprinkle dust on the snoring bear,
Watch him dream and flip, oh my!
While giggling fairies dance in the air.

A feather here, a ribbon there,
Their laughter tickles the morning dew,
As they twirl through skies without a care,
Sharing tales that are old but new.

In that hush, magic skips and plays,
On leaf and twig, their antics flow,
With just a wink, they change the days,
Did you hear that? It's a giggle, you know!

Remnants of Magic in the Air

Lost socks tell tales of wild disguise,
As elves sneak out with a gleam,
They mix up potions not too wise,
And giggle hard over their dream.

Bubble baths turned into clouds,
As they ride on a broomstick high,
Daring each other in funny shrouds,
Cackling like goblins, oh my, oh my!

With shoelaces tied in knots of cheer,
They prance and play, not a care in the world,
Making sprightly jokes to lend an ear,
As whispers of magic around them swirled.

Their world is spun from joyful threads,
Where antics make the stars align,
And laughter dances in tiny spreads,
In the air, where mischief intertwines.

Glimmers of Joy Beneath the Boughs

Beneath the boughs, the giggles bloom,
As little folk plot with great delight,
Their pranks unfold, not a hint of gloom,
A raucous chorus in the night.

With acorns tossed like tiny bombs,
They snag the wrinkles in old chairs,
While faeries craft their dainty psalms,
And sprinkles laughter everywhere.

They juggle stars and tease the moon,
With cheeky grins and playful shouts,
Hiding behind a plump raccoon,
As magic swirls and joy sprout.

In every corner, joy resides,
A kingdom made of fun and flair,
With secrets shared on moonlit tides,
Under boughs where laughter's rare.

The Mischief of Moonlit Shadows

In moonlit nights, they gently play,
Twirling in shadows, they dance away.
With whispers of giggles and laughter so bright,
They stir up mischief till morning light.

With gleeful pranks and a wink of an eye,
They hide in the bushes, oh me, oh my!
Swapping the shoes for a garden hose,
And giggling softly as confusion grows.

They float on the breeze, with a flick of their hats,
Tickling the toes of unsuspecting cats.
With mischievous grins, and a wink so sly,
They turn wooden fences to bounce oh so high.

At dawn's first light, they sneak away,
Leaving only laughter to greet the day.
So if you hear giggles, do not despair,
It's just the elves playing tricks everywhere!

Enchanted Revels of the Fey

Once in a garden, the fairies trot,
In tiny shoes, they dance on the spot.
With petals for skirts and pollen for feast,
They twirl round the daisies, never a beast.

They pop up from tulips, giggle and shout,
"Who's stealing our snacks? Let's figure it out!"
They peek out from roses with eyes open wide,
As the starlit revels unfold in their stride.

With pumpkin pie fights and honeydew games,
They weave little crowns from the fluffiest flames.
Elves sharing jokes with a sparkle so keen,
Making mischief where no one has been.

As night draws near, they fly in a swoop,
Leaving behind a party, a joyfully looped scoop.
Next time you wander through meadows or glens,
Listen for laughter, it starts with the friends!

Laughter Among the Twinkling Leaves

Deep in the forest, where tall trees grow,
Elves tiptoe softly where no one would go.
They giggle and cackle at sight of the moon,
Sprinkling fairy dust with an enchanting tune.

They climb on the branches, with nimble delight,
Swinging on vines as they laugh through the night.
A splash of bright colors, a wink and a cheer,
With pockets of starlust, they draw everyone near.

When autumn leaves flutter, they skip and they twirl,
Turning each leaf into ribbons that swirl.
With playful intentions, and no signs of fear,
They toss all their giggles for all who may hear.

And as dawn approaches, their laughter will fade,
Like the whispers of secrets that twilight once made.
But look for the sparkle where fun lingers still,
For elves will return, with a devious thrill!

The Dance of Dusk and Dawn

As dusk paints the sky in shades of deep blue,
Elves gather 'round with a jubilant crew.
With fireflies dancing and laughter in air,
They twirl in a circle without a care.

With tiny banquets of crumbs and of fruits,
They feast and they frolic in their shining boots.
A sudden loud shout, someone tripped on a toad,
And suddenly giggles spread down the road.

They jump on the mushrooms and swing from the vines,
Playing leapfrog in moonlight, making up lines.
With every new trick, their spirits ignite,
As dawn's golden fingers start tickling the night.

And as the sun rises, the party must cease,
But laughter still lingers, a shining release.
So wherever you wander, keep laughter in sight,
For elves are just waiting to brighten your night!

Glimmers of Magic in the Mist

In the misty morn, they twirl and spin,
Casting light with a cheeky grin.
With tiny feet, they dance around,
Whispering songs, a giggle sound.

They brew up laughter in little pots,
Swapping jokes with the forest tots.
Making mischief, oh what a sight,
Underneath the moon's soft light.

They tickle the flowers and tease the trees,
Hiding behind barks with utmost ease.
Sprinkling giggles on bumblebees,
Creating chaos, just to please.

Oh, the pranks they pull, so sly and smart,
A playful bunch, with a joyful heart.
As day unfolds, their fun won't cease,
A world of magic, full of peace.

Treading Lightly Through Enchanted Places

With whispers soft, they thread the night,
In secret paths, a wondrous sight.
They hop on toadstools, quick and spry,
Crafting giggles as they glide by.

They tiptoe past the sleeping bears,
Sprinkling stardust in the air.
Their laughter rings through leafy trails,
Chasing shadows, lifting tails.

At every turn, a playful snare,
With bouncing sprites and gleeful flair.
In enchanted places, they sway and twirl,
Creating joy with every whirl.

Their mischief blooms like summer flowers,
Counting giggles through the hours.
In moonlit frolic, they take their stance,
Inviting all to join their dance.

The Joys of the Secret Grove

Deep in the woods, where secrets lie,
The tiny folk dance, oh my, oh my!
With glee they skip in the dappled shade,
Painting the leaves with the joy they've made.

They trade their tales with the wandering breeze,
Filling the air with effervescent tease.
In a circle of laughter, they weave their dreams,
Sharing sly winks and whimsical schemes.

Bouncing on mushrooms, they gather round,
In their merry circle, laughter abound.
Creating delights from blossoms and strings,
Oh what a joy, the magic it brings!

Under the stars, they make believe,
That secrets grow on the webs they weave.
In the secret grove, where fun's embraced,
Life's merry moments can never be hast.

Whispers of the Nightshade Elves

In twilight's glow, they start to scheme,
With starlit laughs, they weave their dream.
Hiding among shadows, cheeky and spry,
They share their secrets, with a winked eye.

Nightshade elves whisper in the dark,
Playing tricks with a flicker and spark.
Tickling the moon with a silvery thread,
Swapping tales that dance in your head.

They ride the breezes, swift and light,
Causing giggles before taking flight.
Among the ferns, they play and glide,
Creating laughter, side by side.

As morning breaks, they fade away,
Carrying laughter into the day.
With whispers soft, their fun brings cheer,
A joyful essence that lingers near.

Starlit Adventures in Fairy Realms

Beneath the moon, they dance so bright,
In nightly woods, they take their flight.
With acorn hats and tiny shoes,
They giggle softly, spreading news.

They race the stars, a silly game,
And whisper secrets, cute and lame.
On mushroom stages, they perform,
With every twirl, the night's transformed.

In sparkly streams, they splash about,
Their laughter rings, a merry shout.
They tickle frogs and tease the breeze,
And play hide-and-seek behind the trees.

With firefly lights, they guide the way,
Through shimmering paths where children play.
On puffy clouds, they bounce and soar,
Those little elves, forevermore!

The Delicate Touch of Nature's Hand

With petals soft, they craft a crown,
While bees drone on, they spin around.
They paint the flowers, colors bright,
And giggle when they start a fight.

The squirrels chime in with playful glee,
As elves share snacks made from a tree.
They bake acorn pies with sass,
And teach the ants to do a dance.

At twilight's call, they sneak a peek,
At sleeping blooms, all soft and meek.
They tickle trees with gentle grace,
And send the wind a funny face.

They whisper jokes to passing deer,
Their laughter ringing sweet and clear.
The night's alive with their delight,
As nature giggles, hearts take flight!

Whims of the Woodland Guardians

In leafy halls, they make a fuss,
With breadcrumb trails, giggling thus.
They send the rabbits on wild chases,
And leave behind funny traces.

The owls hoot low, they join the game,
While fireflies gather, full of flame.
With tiny spoons, they stir the night,
Creating tales of pure delight.

They tease the fox, who jumps in fright,
And turn the stars into a kite.
With every prank, the woods obey,
The guardians laugh, come what may.

They cradle dreams in fluffy nests,
And toss the clouds like little jest.
With a wink here, and a nudge there,
They fill the air with silly flair!

Echoes of Laughter in Emerald Fields

At dawn's soft touch, they start to play,
In fields of green, they joke all day.
With hopscotch stones and dandelion,
They leap and bound, no caring fun.

They catch the breeze on silly swings,
And paint the sky with giggling flings.
With twinkling eyes, they set the scene,
For merry tales of what's unseen.

In burrows deep, they hide and peep,
With dragonflies, they laugh and leap.
While daisies dance to secret tunes,
They weave bright plans beneath the moons.

The sun dips low, a golden hue,
As sleepy flowers bid adieu.
In emerald fields, their echoes flow,
A legacy of joy to sow!

Secrets of the Sparkling Glens

In the glens where laughter rings,
Elves are up to silly things.
They hide the shoes and mix the socks,
And dance around like little flocks.

With tiny hats and sneaky grins,
They plot and plan their playful spins.
A pinch of dust, a wiggle here,
And suddenly the cats all cheer!

They sprinkle joy in every nook,
With tricks as clever as a storybook.
A giggle here, a giggle there,
The glens are filled with magic flair.

So if you hear a twinkle sound,
Remember, joy is all around.
In the sparkling glens, oh so bright,
Elves spread laughter, day and night.

Twilight Mischief and Midnight Wonders

As twilight falls, the elves awake,
They stir the pot, they love to bake.
With cookies gone and flour in hair,
They giggle under the moon's glare.

Their pranks are sweet and oftentimes mean,
Like hiding spoons where no one's seen.
A sprinkle here, a dash of that,
They turn a puppy into a cat!

Underneath the starlit skies,
They chase the shadows, oh what a surprise!
With firefly lights in bouncy bounds,
Their laughter echoes all around.

If night falls quiet, don't you fear,
For mischief brews when elves are near.
In midnight wonders, fun delights,
Elves weave mischief and starry nights.

The Craft of Light and Shadow

With twinkling eyes and nimble hands,
Elves craft magic in wild lands.
They giggle soft, their whispers low,
Creating shadows that dance and glow.

They twirl and spin, a playful sight,
Mixing shadow with beams of light.
A flicker here, a flare of cheer,
"Oh look, a goblin! Quick, my dear!"

Their crafts are odd, their art unique,
With silly shapes that make you squeak.
A goblet full of rainbow trends,
"Oh, look! It's talking! It pretends!"

So if you wander in twilight's hold,
You may spot elves, brave and bold.
With light and shadow, fun they weave,
And in their craft, you'll laugh and believe.

Guardians of Forgotten Stories

In cozy nooks with stories tall,
Elves guard the tales, both big and small.
With every page, a giggle brews,
As socks talk back and pies refuse!

They swap the endings when you're asleep,
And add some chaos to tales that creep.
"Once upon a time," they cheerfully say,
"A dragon lost his pants today!"

With every fable, they weave delight,
Twisting old truths from day to night.
In forgotten stories, laughter flows,
As elves embrace the joy that glows.

So when you open a book to read,
Remember, elves plant mischief seeds.
Guardians of tales, they're never far,
Turning tales into giggles, oh how bizarre!

The Hidden Crafts of the Fey Folk

In shadows deep, they weave with glee,
With twinkling threads of mystery.
They stitch the dreams of sleepy heads,
And wrap them tight in mossy beds.

They craft the laughter of the streams,
And catch the sighs of willow dreams.
With tiny tools made just for fun,
They shape the joy of everyone.

In splashes bright, the colors dance,
They paint the air with whimsy's glance.
With giggles sweet, the fey unite,
To make the world a pure delight.

So if you hear a faint, soft cheer,
It's just the fey folk drawing near.
They sprinkle magic, light, and cheer,
While sipping dew and holding beer!

Celestial Charms and Forest Jewels

In each small glen, a shimmer glows,
With trinkets made of leaves and bows.
They trade for stars, with acorn caps,
And giggle softly at their mishaps.

With mossy crowns atop their heads,
They dance on toadstools, scatter spreads.
They barter charms with passing sun,
And chase the clouds just for the fun.

They hitch a ride on breezy dreams,
With spinning tops and silver beams.
Their laughter rings through bramble thorns,
As twilight sings and daylight scorns.

These little folk, with heart so bold,
Wear sunny smiles, not just the gold.
Their treasures are the silly games,
And friendship's glow, which never wanes!

Enigma of the Moonlit Path

Beneath the moon, they twirl and sway,
With whispers light, they turn to play.
They ride on fireflies, soft and bright,
Transforming shadows into light.

In every step, a riddle found,
With giggly hints that swirl around.
They hide behind each twisting tree,
And laugh at mortals who can't see.

The path they weave is full of cheer,
With winking stars and nightingale near.
They toss confetti made of mist,
And tease the moon, none can resist!

So stroll along the hidden ways,
And catch the fey in merry play.
With joyful hearts, they tip their hat,
Inviting all to join their chat!

Twilight's Whisper Among the Trees

When twilight falls, the fey awake,
With tinkling bells and laughter's shake.
They weave a story, row by row,
As fireflies dance in evening's glow.

They tickle ferns and swirl the leaves,
With secret games that no one perceives.
In every rustle, there's a jest,
As leaves conspire to play their best.

A nighttime feast of berries sweet,
With mugwort cakes and shimm'ring treats.
They raise a toast to foolish fun,
And spin in circles 'til they're done.

So if you hear a chuckle near,
It's just the fey folk drawing near.
They spin the tales of night with glee,
A hidden world for you and me!

The Boon of the Twilight Hours

In the twilight glow, they prance with glee,
Sprinkling laughter like confetti on a tree.
With tiny hats and shoes that twinkle bright,
They dance in circles, a comical sight.

They juggle acorns and skip along streams,
Whispering secrets of dream-filled themes.
Telling tales of hiccuping frogs and snails,
While crafting wands from tangled fairy trails.

With doughnut-shaped clouds, they float and glide,
Sipping on sunshine, with joy as their guide.
In every nook, a giggle or two,
These silly sprites have their own rendezvous.

When the moonlight spills, the mischief ignites,
Painting the night with their playful delights.
So join the fun, and laugh till you ache,
For in these twilight hours, giggles never break.

Echoes of Magic in Every Leaf

Beneath the boughs, they sing and they sway,
Rustling the leaves in a cheeky ballet.
With each little giggle, the branches all shake,
As squirrels join in for a nutty cake break.

Their whispers tickle the quivering grass,
A tick-tock dance that will never pass.
From acorns to daisies, they take immense pride,
In crafting concoctions that bubble and slide.

They paint rainbows on puddles, with glee in their eyes,
While offering chocolate to passing blue flies.
With pockets of giggles and hats made of air,
They weave threads of magic without a care.

So if you stroll past, be careful, take care,
Their laughter might catch you, leading to dare.
And who knows, perhaps, you'll join in their play,
As echoes of magic brighten your day.

Melody of the Hidden Glens

In hidden glens where the daisies bloom,
A band of rascals makes chatter and zoom.
They hum to the flowers, they croon to the trees,
Tickling the breezes like a cheeky tease.

Each note they sing brings the butterflies near,
Twisting and twirling, spreading giggles and cheer.
With wands made of whimsy, they conjure delight,
Creating a party that lasts through the night.

They tickle the toads till they jump off their logs,
And play tag with shadows as they chase the frogs.
With petal-capped hats, they bounce and they sway,
While the stars watch closely, joining their play.

So if you stumble upon this secretive scene,
Prepare for a ruckus, a fun-loving team.
For the melody sings in a way so divine,
That laughter and magic forever entwine.

Crafting Wonders in the Realm of Dreams

In the realm of dreams, they gather at night,
Knitting the wishes, making futures bright.
With shimmering threads from starry delight,
They weave all the giggles till morning's first light.

They're baking up shortcakes with frosting so sweet,
But accidentally add some peculiar beet.
With a splash and a pop, the concoctions take flight,
Leaving trails of chuckles that dance in the night.

With a puff of their cheeks, and a wink or a grin,
They conjure balloon animals that bounce in.
Nose-picking gnomes giggle at silly sight,
As mischief unfolds, gleefully slight.

So dreamers beware, when the clocks strike the hour,
The elves are out crafting with magic and power.
And if you are lucky, you just might receive,
A sprinkle of laughter, a dream to believe.

Guardians of Woodland Whimsy

In moonlit nights, they tap dance in glee,
With acorn hats and shoes made of leaves.
They tickle the squirrels and share cups of tea,
While weaving tall tales that nobody believes.

With laughter that jingles like wind chimes in spring,
They sprinkle bright stardust on every shoe.
In secretive meetings, they plot and they sing,
Of mischief and magic—a party for two.

They race through the shadows, swift as a breeze,
Stealing the sunlight for fun on a dare.
With nibbles of fungus, they feast on the trees,
Playing hide and seek in the wild woodland lair.

As dawn starts to break, they vanish from sight,
Leaving behind giggles and whispers of cheer.
In twilight they frolic, oh what a delight,
Guardians of whimsy, forever sincere.

Crafting Dreams with Gossamer Threads

In the heart of the glen, they stitch clouds with care,
Using gossamer threads that shimmer and shine.
They sew up the giggles, the dreams float up there,
Befriending the stars, one twinkle at a time.

With needles of starlight, they craft tales of fun,
Whispering secrets to each daffodil.
A dash of mischief, a sprinkle of sun,
Sewing bright wishes will be their finest skill.

From velvet horizons, they harvest the mirth,
And stitch it in patterns of laughter divine.
With every creation, they prove their worth,
Crafting sweet dreams where whimsy aligns.

As dawn starts to dawn, they pack up their wares,
Leaving behind a quilt of delight.
In the forest of wonders, they scatter their cares,
And vanish like whispers, all hidden from sight.

Beneath the Canopy of Elysium

Beneath leafy boughs, where sunlight streams in,
They play fiddle tunes with a sparkly flair.
Bouncing on mushrooms, they giggle and spin,
With laughter that dances in the warm, scented air.

A game of hide and seek 'round the old twisted oak,
Where shadows twist lightly, and secrets ensue.
They whisper to flowers, each juvenile joke,
And the bees buzz along, joining the crew.

They dabble in wonders, painting the skies,
With flakes of bright magic, they shimmer and whirl.
Creating the colors of laughter and sighs,
As butterflies flutter, they spin and they twirl.

When moonbeams arrive, they break out the sweets,
With nectar and honey, a feast to excite.
The night full of magic, and merry heartbeats,
Beneath the grand canopy, pure joy ignites.

Songs of the Silver-barked Trees

In whispers so soft, they sing to the trees,
Charming the branches with giggles and twine.
They craft leafy melodies, swaying with ease,
As echoes of laughter bounce back through the pine.

Under silver-barked trunks, they twirl in delight,
Dancing with shadows that flicker and flee.
With a hop and a skip, they banter all night,
Sipping on raindrops, oh what a spree!

From starlit high notes to whispers below,
They serenade moonbeams like soft, flowing streams.
In a symphony born of pure joyous flow,
They hold curious secrets and magical dreams.

And as daylight creeps in, they vanish from sight,
Leaving echoes of laughter that linger and stay.
When twilight returns, they emerge in the light,
To sing to the silver-barked trees every day.

Dance of the Silver-Haired Kin

In a clearing where moonlight sways,
Silver-haired kin come out to play.
They twirl and spin with such delight,
Chasing shadows through the night.

With giggles that ripple like a stream,
Their laughter's a mischievous dream.
They trip on roots and tumble down,
Rolling like clouds, no hint of frown.

They step in flowers, they leap in glee,
Beneath the branches of a grand oak tree.
In their silliness, joy takes flight,
As creatures all watch, hearts feel light.

When dawn arrives, they vanish fast,
Leaving whispers of fun, a spell they've cast.
With silver hair caught in the breeze,
They promise to return, if you please.

Secrets of the Enchanted Forge

In a forge where sparkles fly,
Elves with hammers laugh and sigh.
They craft the oddest, wittiest things,
Like musical spoons that chirp and sing.

With armor made of shiny cheese,
They work with joy, they work with ease.
A wheezy old dragon breathes a puff,
And elves just giggle, 'Oh, that's enough!'

They melt down wishes and sprinkle dreams,
Creating mishaps, bursting seams.
A boot that dances, a sword that squeaks,
In their strange world, laughter peaks.

When orders come for fiery foes,
They chuckle and say, 'That's not how it goes!'
With whimsy and wonders, their creations roar,
A jolly brigade, forevermore.

Shadows Play Among the Pines

When shadows creep through trees so tall,
Elfin giggles echo, a playful call.
They chase the light with silly grace,
With clumsy hops and a grin on each face.

Beneath the pines, they hide and seek,
With twinkling eyes, they peek and squeak.
Jumping out from bushes, they shout, 'Boo!'
Then tumble and roll, all covered in dew.

They juggle acorns, and spin around,
Crashing softly onto the ground.
With silly songs sung in the breeze,
They leave the forest swaying with ease.

At dusk, they gather, a raucous throng,
Swapping tall tales and dancing along.
With shadows stretching, they bid goodnight,
But not before causing more delight.

Laughter Echoes in the Glimmering Grove

In the glimmering grove, where fireflies waltz,
Elves share secrets, giggles, and faults.
With mischievous grins, they set up a show,
Letting the wild tales mischievously flow.

One claims a mushroom can fly with flair,
Another insists it's a seat for a bear.
They burst out laughing at the silliest things,
As the moon blinks down and the night softly sings.

With dance steps so quirky, they spin in their ways,
Chasing the moonbeams through soft, shimm'ring rays.
They leap over logs, trip over roots,
Squeaking with joy in their silly cute boots.

As the stars twinkle bright, they whisper goodbyes,
Leaving behind a trail of wide-eyed surprise.
In the morning sun, their laughter will rise,
Bringing back mirth to the brightening skies.

Harmony in Nature's Hidden Melodies

In the forest, they hide and play,
Tickling the leaves, making them sway.
With a wink and a giggle, they sing,
Bringing joy to the tiniest spring.

They ride on the backs of bright butterflies,
Whispering secrets, exchanging sly sighs.
In mushroom cap boats, they float on the dew,
Making funny faces as they drift through.

Under the roots, they dance and tease,
Crafting mischief with amusing ease.
They sprinkle the earth with glittery dust,
Promising laughter is a must!

By moonlight, they twirl in a merry spree,
Chasing the shadows, as happy as can be.
With a flash of their smiles, the world they adorn,
In nature's chuckle, a new dawn is born.

The Sorcery of Starlit Skies

Beneath the stars, in the midnight air,
Elves concoct laughter, with utmost care.
They brew up giggles in cauldrons wide,
Stirring delight with a flick and glide.

A comet's tail becomes a slippery slide,
While moonbeam trails add to their pride.
Shooting stars, like sprinkles, they toss,
In the game of hide and seek, they are the boss.

With cupcakes that float in the cosmic spree,
They munch on wishes, as sweet as can be.
Between the twinkles, a waltz they dance,
In the realm of the cosmos, they take a chance.

As dawn approaches, the giggles will fade,
But the tales of their tricks will never degrade.
They'll scatter the joy with a wink of the eye,
For even in slumber, the fun will not die.

Enchantment at the Edge of Dawn

At first light, with grins wide and bright,
Elves juggle dreams in the early light.
Whispering wishes and playful schemes,
Crafting the sweetest of morning dreams.

They tickle the flowers to bloom with glee,
While butterflies giggle, "Come play with me!"
With the sun rays dancing, they race in a line,
Painting the world in colors divine.

Sipping on nectar from blossoms so sweet,
They stomp in puddles, a splashy feat.
Every droplet a note in their joyous song,
In the symphony of laughter, they truly belong.

As the day unfurls, their pranks will ignite,
Leaving trails of giggles in morning light.
In every corner, their magic will sway,
For laughter is pure, come what may.

Citadels of Joy Among the Glades

In the glades, they dance and prance,
Creating mischief at every chance.
With hats so tall, and shoes that squeak,
They giggle and hide, they'll never peak.

Under moonlight, they play their songs,
Building giggle forts, oh how it throngs!
With acorn cups and berry pies,
Their laughter bubbles under smiling skies.

Squirrels join in with a cheeky cheer,
While raccoons wink, oh so sincere.
They sprinkle joy with every twirl,
In their world, it's a funny swirl.

With mischief managed, they call it a day,
And in their dreams, they frolic and sway.
For joy is treasure found in the leaves,
Where elves reside and laughter weaves.

Whirlwind of Elfin Dreams

Whirling around in a playful spree,
Elves zip and zoom past the old oak tree.
They borrow moonlight to light the way,
And ride on the backs of the breezy day.

Tiny voices echo with giggles and squeals,
As they plot sweet tricks with enchanted feels.
A concoction of giggles and sprightly tunes,
They tickle the trees and dance with the moons.

When the stars twinkle, it's time for a race,
They leap through the air with such elfin grace.
Sprinkling sparkles, they draw on the night,
Mixing mischief until morning light.

With a snap and a clap, their fun has begun,
Turning sighs into smiles for everyone.
In a whirlwind of dreams, they spread pure delight,
These cheeky little sprites make everything bright.

Guardians of the Sunbeam Trail

On the sunbeam trail, they gather in fun,
Playing chase with shadows till the day is done.
With tiny bows and laughter so loud,
They play hide and seek amid the crowd.

Keeping watch with a wink and a nudge,
They tickle the flowers and never judge.
With a gust of wind, they steal a kiss,
As butterflies whirl in sheer bliss.

Their guardian giggles echo like bells,
As they weave their magic with playful spells.
Sprinkling light where the daisies sway,
Each day is a carnival in frolic and play.

Amid the trees, with a flip and a flap,
They spin tales of fun, while taking a nap.
For laughter and joy are the paths they trail,
These merry keepers of the sunbeam trail.

Crystals and Cloaks in the Mysterious Woods

In the woods where shadows play and scheme,
Elves wear crystals that twinkle and gleam.
With cloaks that shimmer, they sneak and peek,
At the antics of critters who giggle and squeak.

They plot their tricks with mischief in mind,
While mushrooms dance and the fireflies bind.
A splash of joy with a sprinkle of cheer,
Their silly antics bring laughter near.

With stardust caught in their twinkling eyes,
They bounce through the ferns, their laughter flies.
Building castles in air, they dream up delight,
In a cloak of giggles that fills up the night.

And when dawn breaks, like bubbles they float,
Elves vanish like mist, their giggles remote.
But their humor remains, like the sun's warm rays,
In the heart of the woods, where joy always stays.

Mystical Fables of the Forest Elders

In the twilight glen, so dim and bright,
Elders gather round, a curious sight.
They tickle the roots and juggle the air,
With mushroom hats that they proudly wear.

Squirrels giggle, a band of their own,
As the wise ones toss acorns, skills they've honed.
With whispers of magic, they swap tall tales,
Of mischievous sprites and their wild gales.

A fox joins in with a dance so spry,
While bats spin around, aiming for the sky.
The moon peeks through, both gleeful and sly,
As laughter rings out, floating up high.

When dawn creeps in, they scamper away,
Leaving behind echoes of their play.
In the heart of the woods, charm never dies,
Just secrets and giggles beneath the skies.

The Dance of Leaves and Laughter

Leaves swirl and twirl in the morning breeze,
Elves giggle and tease, with unmatched ease.
They play hide and seek with shadows of trees,
Crafting crowns of daisies, as light drips like honey.

With acorn-shaped drums, they tap a sweet song,
The rhythm ignites, and they all dance along.
A fox in a vest joins the jubilant throng,
While chipmunks applaud, "Oh, you can't go wrong!"

Sprinkling dew drops, they paint the sky blue,
Creating a rainbow, just for a few.
They giggle so loudly, the echoes break through,
The sun shines brighter; oh, what a view!

As night falls softly, they turn in to rest,
With dreams of tomorrow, they are truly blessed.
In a world full of joy, they give it their best,
For life's just a dance, a whimsical quest.

The Celestial Playground of the Fey

In realms where giggles ring like a bell,
The fey fly and flip, casting a spell.
With sparkles and whispers, they twirl through the night,
Playing hopscotch on stars, a marvelous sight.

A bumblebee band leads a merry parade,
As daisies and dandelions all join in spade.
The clouds join the fun, forming shapes out of dream,
While laughter erupts like a bubbling stream.

Fairies brew potions in shiny glass jugs,
Mixing bright colors with giggles and hugs.
With winks and bright grins, they charm every bug,
Creating a ruckus, sweet mischief in plugs.

As dawn's golden fingers brush past their play,
The fey float away, till the close of the day.
For each night is a feast, where they frolic and sway,
In the celestial playground, where joy finds a way.

Curiosities of the Hidden Realm

Behind every tree where the wildberries grow,
Elves tinker and craft in a shimmering glow.
With jars filled with stardust, they brew strange delights,
Turning sleepy toads into dancing sprites.

They set sail on leaves, through pools like blue glass,
With weathered maps drawn in crayon and sass.
They giggle at squirrels, their whiskers askew,
As they plot zany plans that are absolutely new.

Each night brings a riddle, a quest to unfold,
With laughter and joy, in this world made of gold.
Like stories of old, where the fun never ends,
Adventures await in the realm where joy bends.

So peek through the shadows, don't let it go past,
Join in on their games, make the fun ever last.
In the curiosities where giggles are cast,
Life's sweetness is endless; the spell's ever vast.

Milton Keynes UK
Ingram Content Group UK Ltd.
UKHW021927011224
451790UK00005B/54

9 789916 908488